Jobs For Today's Economy:
Work From Home Manual©

Copyright © 2018 George Publishing Inc.

www.georgepublishing.com
www.jobs42day.com
248-955-3145

This book, or parts thereof, may not be reproduced in any form without permission from the publisher.

Written by Jennifer Benson

ISBN# 978-0-615-87678-8

Table of Contents

Introduction	i
Working-from-home overview	1
Work-from-home equipment	6
Work-from-home job search tips	9
Work-from-home employer websites	12
Entrepreneurship	47
Job searching tips	54
Resume writing tips	57
Traditional careers in-demand	62

Introduction

My name is Jennifer Benson. Since 2001, I've been working-from-home doing a variety of jobs, including secret shopping, customer service, inventory control and other contractual work for different companies. In addition, I own and operate a publishing business and a nonprofit organization. I love working-from-home, because I'm my own boss, I set my own schedule, I'm in charge of my income and I don't have to leave my home.

When I first started working-from-home, I worked a traditional job and worked from home part-time. However, in 2006, when I started my family, I realized that it would be more beneficial to work-from-home fulltime.

My first work-from-home job was as a Mortgage Closing Agent. From there, I started researching other ways to make money while working-from-home. I've managed to maintain over ten different work-from-home contracts/jobs. Here is a short list of some of the companies that I've partnered and/or worked with:

1. Westathome
2. Concentrix
3. GCS Field Research
4. BDS Marketing
5. DSG Associates
6. Convergys
7. Liveops
8. NotaryPro
9. Service Intelligence
10. Ellis Property Management
11. Bare International

12. Virtual Works

13. iSecretShop

14. United States Census Bureau

And many more.

I'm often asked how I work-from-home and how can people get started? These questions are answered in this book. In addition to discussing the work-from-home industry, this book is an overall career guide.

This book is about different ways to earn income. I will touch on being an entrepreneur, independent contractor, and traditional employment that is in demand.

If you are interested in earning more money, you should be diligent in pursuing more money. Take at least two to three hours per day researching, planning, submitting resumes, job applications and developing ways that you can successfully reach your financial goals. There are many ways to earn money and you can earn that money as an employee, independent contractor, entrepreneur or all three.

Being a **traditional employee** is a great way to earn income. You work when your boss schedules you. You may receive health insurance benefits, 401(k) plans, and some stock options. You pay into social security for your retirement and your employer makes sure you pay your taxes. There are some great perks with being an employee. Having a traditional job isn't for everyone. Some individuals have a passion for self-employment.

An **independent contractor** is a person and/or company that completes projects or assignments for companies. Independent contractors can make the most money in the shortest amount of time and companies pay them. An independent contractor's schedule is flexible, and they work with little to no supervision. Being an independent contractor is like being an entrepreneur because you are the boss. A company is paying you for your products and services. The main difference between a contractor and an entrepreneur is that you are working on the behalf of someone else. One major benefit about being an independent contractor is that the funds are reliable and steady. Contractors are responsible for paying their own taxes and are 1099 instead of W-2, when filing taxes with the IRS. If the independent contractor keeps a good reputation, the company that contracts them will continue to work with them. Your reputation and work ethic are the keys to keeping your contracts.

An **entrepreneur** is the most rewarding way to generate wealth. You are 100% the boss, you manage your schedule, and your employees' schedules. Things are done the way you want, when you want, and how you want. You are paid to do what you are passionate about. You are solely responsible for your income, paying taxes and planning for your retirement. We will discuss entrepreneurship in more detail on page 47.

How do you currently earn your income?

- Are you an employee?
- Independent contractor?
- An entrepreneur?
- Are you more than one?

Which one would you prefer?

The first topic we will discuss is working-from-home and the companies that will hire you. We will touch on entrepreneurship and executing your business plan. Then we will discuss traditional employment, job searching, resume writing and jobs that are in demand. The resources provided in this book will help you reach your professional goals, whether you want a full-time job, want to work-from-home, supplement your income or change careers. Let us discuss working-from-home.

I ♥
Working from home!

Working-From-Home

The Work-From-Home industry is thriving like never before. Many companies are changing the way they hire their employees. Employers no longer want to pay for health insurance, equipment, and employee overhead costs. Therefore, many companies are shifting from hiring fulltime employees to hiring independent contractors and work-from-home agents.

There are many work-from-home industries ranging from customer service, marketing, secret shopping, and web design, to name a few. Customer service is the number one work-from-home industry. Customer service is a good industry to get started working-from-home because companies are always hiring for customer service and sales positions. Income may vary from your state's minimum wage to a six-figure income. It is whatever you make it. You can work as little or as much as you like. You can hold as many contracts/jobs with as many companies as you can handle. The great thing is that some companies will let you set your own schedule. So, if you manage your time right, you will be on the road to making the money you always wanted to make.

Working-from-home is not for everyone. Not everyone can handle working without a supervisor. Some have found themselves either overwhelmed or underutilized. With that being said, let us determine if working-from-home is right for you:

1). <u>Do you have good problem-solving skills?</u>
You will be working independently and if a problem and/or question arises, you must be able to handle it quickly with little to no help.

2). <u>How are your time management skills?</u>

Deadlines must be met, and work should be completed in a timely manner. Good time management is a plus. No procrastination allowed!

3). <u>Can you work independently, with no supervision?</u>

No one will remind you to work, punch a clock or maintain your schedule. You must be a self-starter.

4). <u>Do you have good multi-tasking skills?</u>
Being able to listen, while researching, and inputting data is important. Being able to handle more than one project will earn you more money.

5). <u>Do you have great customer service and communication abilities?</u>

Clear and concise communication is helpful. Being able to handle and defuse an irate customer without being easily upset is a characteristic of a good customer service representative and entrepreneur.

6). <u>Are you organized?</u>

Having good organizational skills will keep your home business running smoothly.

7). <u>Are you willing to give up the camaraderie of the work place?</u>

You will be working independently with no co-workers. You may have some virtual co-workers that you can communicate with.

8). <u>Can you maintain your income</u>?

You will oversee your income. If you do not work, you do not get paid.

Is working-from-home right for you? Keep in mind that being a contractor or work-from-home employee, you are representing a company and you must be knowledgeable of their products, services, policies and procedures.

Now, let us discuss what equipment you might need to be successful at your new work-from-home career.

Equipment Needed to Work-From-Home

The listed equipment is not mandatory for all jobs/contracts. Yet, these items are beneficial if you are an entrepreneur. Some companies may prefer that you have the listed equipment:

1) A computer, a desktop or laptop.

2) Internet connection, Hardwire DSL or Cable high-speed service.

3) Basic landline telephone services, with a phone that has a hands-free-headset connection.

4) Miscellaneous office items you may need:
   - Fax machine
   - Printer
   - Tablet
   - Smart phone

These items are not required and may be accumulated over time. You don't have to get internet, telephone service, or any other equipment immediately. You can wait until you obtain a job/contract before you make these commitments. In the meantime, you can utilize your local library's resources until you find employment. Some companies may send you the necessary equipment needed for your job functions.

Since the work-from-home industry is so broad, there is no set pay rate. Some companies may pay you per minute, per hour, or per job. Companies can pay you your state's minimum wage or they can pay you a yearly salary. It all depends on the company you work for and the position, contract or assignments you prefer. Still, working-from-home does save you time and money. With the increasing costs of childcare, gas, food and not being able to spend time with your family, working-from-home might be right for you. Depending on your lifestyle, you could save approximately $910.00 per month working-from-home. Here are some approximate calculations:

Gas $40 per week for a month	$160
Lunch, $5 per day, for a month	$100
Daycare if needed for a month	$650
No more rush hour commute, priceless!	$0
Approximate total monthly savings	$910

There maybe other miscellaneous expenses you may incur daily, weekly, monthly and yearly in the workplace. How much do you spend going to work every month?

Lunch: _____

Gas: _____

Daycare: _____

Clothes: _____

Travel time: _____

Other expenses: _____

_____

Work-From-Home Search Tips

An important tip when searching work-from-home job opportunities is knowing the terminology employers use to describe work-from-home positions. Some terms that may be used are:

- remote,
- telecommute,
- virtual office,
- work from home,
- home office,
- home based,
- virtual agent,
- virtual office,
- freelance,
- submission,
- contractor,
- offsite

Be aware of these phrases when searching work-from-home employment. You can type these words into the keyword search on the company's job search page. Make sure you type these terms into the keyword search and not the location search for better results.

Don't limit yourself to only searching the companies listed in this book. Many companies are hiring work-from-home agents, and independent contractors. Search any company you come across, ones you are familiar with, and the ones you are unfamiliar with. Use the above key words when searching. Good luck on your work-from-home job search.

Work-From-Home Employers

Listed are some work-from-home industries, companies and their websites. Find which industry/industries that best suit you by evaluating your skills, experience and education. Most of the companies listed will provide you with the necessary training and company software to be successful while working. Some of the companies listed hire independent contractors and/or employees. Browse the company's website and career page for more information and to apply for work-from-home opportunities. Review the resumé writing section on page 57 so you can submit your best resumé to your future work-from-home employer.

Let us get started searching for a work-from-home job. The industries are listed in alphabetical order, good luck.

Accounting and Finance

Positions in this category include bookkeepers, accountants, financial planners, account consultants, tax preparers and other finance positions.

Company Name	Website
Accounting Department	accountingdepartment.com
Bateman & Co., Inc	batemanhouston.com
Bookminders	bookminders.com
Enterprise Recovery Sys. Inc	ersinc.com
First Data	firstdata.com
Virtual Accountants	virtualaccountants.com
Bid a Wiz	bidawiz.com
CEO Ventures	ceoventures.com
Corptax	corptax.com
York	yorkrsg.com
Intuit	intuit.com
Price Water House Coopers	pwc.com
Smart Books	smartbookscorp.com
TAD Accounting	tadaccounting.com

Arts, Craft and Assemblers

Companies in this category hire or contract freelance artists, photographers, graphic designers, and assemblers.

Company Name	Website
The Bradford Group	thebradfordgroup.com
Cricket	cricketmedia.com
Analog Science Fiction	analogsf.com
American Greetings	americangreetings.com
Excel Sportswear	exceltees.com
ArtFire	artfire.com
Blue Mountain Arts	sps.com
Assemblers Inc.,	assemblersinc.net
La Bella Baskets	forever.labellabaskets.com
Art Fire	artfire.com
Oatmeal Studios Greeting Cards	oatmealstudios.com
CafePress	cafepress.com
Avatar Press	avatarpress.com
Shutter Stock	shutterstock.com
Create My Tattoo	createmytattoo.com
Leanin' Tree	leanintree.com

Rubber Stamp Madness	rsmadness.com
Wild Apple	wildapple.com
Etsy	etsy.com
Tee Spring	teespring.com
Handy.com	handy.com
Dolly	dolly.com
GoShare	goshare.co
Your Mechanic	yourmechanic.com
We Go Look	wegolook.com
Zaarly	zaarly.com

Authors/Writers

The companies below hire or contract individuals with different backgrounds in writing and editing.

Company Name	Website
Analog Science Fiction	analogsf.com
Appingo	appingo.com
Funny Times	funnytimes.com
Just Answer	justanswer.com
Maven Research	maven.co
Chegg	chegg.com

Performancing	performancing.com
EduWriters	eduwriters.com
Expert Tutors	experttutors.com
Avanti	avantipress.com
Topics Education	topicseducation.com
Aria Communications	ariacallsandcards.com
The Sun Magazine	rsmadness.com
Investigative Reporters and Editors	ire.org
Proof Read Now	proofreadnow.com
KGB Answers	542542.com
Scribendi	scribendi.com
Write On Results	writeonresults.com
Webster Tech Writers	techwriters.com
Academic Word	academicword.com
Blue Mountain Arts	sps.com
Sierra	sierraclub.org
Thesis & Dissertation Advisor	dissertationadvisors.com
Tech Writers	techwriters.com
Text Broker	textbroker.com
Managed Editing	managedediting.com

| Writers Weekly | writersweekly.com |

Court Reporting

This list includes, mock juries, court researchers, court reporters, individuals that conduct background checks, and more.

Company Name	Website
Alderson Court Reporting	aldersonreporting.com
Advanced Background Check	abcheck.com
Back Ground Profiles	backgroundprofiles.com
Hire Right	hireright.com
First National Bank	fnba.com
SunLark Research	sunlarkresearch.com
Vicky's Virtual Receptionist	vickyvirtual.com
Integrity Title Records	integritytitlerecords.com
WolfGang Research	wolfgangresearch.com
Counsel Oncall	counseloncall.com
E.P. Dine	epdine.com
e Jury	ejury.com
Online Verdicts	onlineverdict.com

Accurate Background Inc	accuratebackground.com
Validity Screening Solutions	validityscreening.com
Data Quest LTD	dataquest.co
Deed Collector	deedcollector.com
JBS Court Research Service	work4jbs.com

Customer Service

These companies hire/contract individuals with a background in the call center environment. These positions consist of inbound and/or out bound calls for sales, technical support and customer service.

Company Name	**Website**
Service 800	service800inc.com
Sutherland Global Service	sutherlandathome.com
TeleTech	hirepoint.com
Uhaul	uhaul.com
Pleio	goodstartu.info
XAct Telesolutions	myxact.com
Century Link	centurylink.com
Transcom	transcom.com

Convergys	convergys.com
American Support	americansupport.com
Working Solutions	workingsolutions.com
Arise	arise.com
VIP Desk	vipdesk.com
Intrep Sales Partners	intrep.com
Liveops	liveops.com
Next Level Solutions	dial-nls.com
Neiman Marcus	neimanmarcus.com
On Point Advocacy	onpointathome.com
Apple	apple.com
Concentrix	concentrix.com
Nordstrom	shop.nordstrom.com
Craft Coffee	craftcoffee.com
castle branch	castlebranch.com
Metaverse Mod Squad	metaversemodsquad.com
Mcgraw Hill	mheducation.com
RBS Citzens Financial Group	cfgcareers.com
Adecco	adeccousa.com
Accolade Support	accoladesupport.com

Amazon	us-amazon.icims.com
American Airlines	careers.aa.com
Alorica	alorica.com
ARO	callcenteroptions.com
Best Western Hotel	bestwestern.com
COX	cox.com
cruise.com	cruise.com
Stella Service INC	stellaservice.com
Direct Interactions	directinteractions.com
Expert Planet	expertplanet.com
Front Line Call Center	frontlinecallcenter.com
General Electric	ge.com
Globe Wired	globewired.com
Great Virtual Work	greatvirtualworks.com
Weebly	careers.weebly.com
Hilton Hotel	hiltonworldwide.com
Home Shopping Network	hsn.com
Ipsos	ipsos-na.com
Maritz Research	maritzresearch.com
MicahTek, Inc.	micahtek.com

NCO	ncogroup.com
NexRep	nexrep.com
Site Staff	sitestaff.com
Smart Office Solutions	smartofficesolutions.com
SiTel	sitel.com
Starwood Hotels	starwoodhotels.com
Ver-A-Fast Corporation	verafast.net
Dell	Dell.com
American express	americanexpress.com
Pitney Bowes	pitneybowes.com
Welcome Wagon	welcomewagon.com
Enterprise Contact Center	go.enterpriseholdings.com
American Heart Association	heart.org
Bausch & Lomb	bausch.com
SumTotal Systems	sumtotalsystems.com
Ecolab	ecolab.com
Xerox	xerox.com
Forest Laboratories	frx.com
Symantec	symantec.com
Teradata Corporation	teradata.com

Company Name	Website
TEK Systems	teksystems.com
Lockheed Martin	lockheedmartin.com
Microsoft	microsoft.com
Mom Corps	momcorps.com
ACI Group	aci.com
Wonder	askwonder.com
VOIQ	voiq.com

Captioners /Stenographers

Captioners or Stenographers type audio into text for television programming and legal depositions.

Company Name	Website
Caption Colorado	captioncolorado.com
Vitac	vitac.com
Vanan Captioning	vanancaptioning.com
Phillips Reporting	phippsreporting.com
Rev	rev.com
Tiger Fish	tigerfish.com
Babble Type	babbletype.com
Wordz Xpressed	wordzx.com
BSG	bsgclearing.com

Maritz Cx	maritzcx.com

Education

This includes online professors, tutors and other instructional positions.

Company Name	Website
Limu	limu.com
Parliament Tutors	parliamenttutors.com
Berlitz	berlitz.us
Straighterline	straighterline.com
Tutor.com	tutor.com
Universal Class	universalclass.com
UC Berkeley Extension	extension.berkeley.edu
Western Governors University	wgu.edu
California Virtual Academies	cava.k12.com
Wyz Ant Tutoring	wyzant.com
Academic Word	academicword.com
AIM for A	aim4a.com

American Intercontinental University	careers.aiuonline.edu
Bilingual America	bilingualamerica.com
Chronicle of Higher Education	chroniclevitae.com
Educational Testing Service	ets.org
Brainfuse	brainfuse.com
Homework Help	homeworkhelp.com
Homework Tutoring	homeworktutoring.com
TNTP	tntp.org
Connection Academy	connectionsacademy.com
Amplify	amplify.com
Expert Tutor	experttutors.com
Walden University	waldenu.edu
Kaplan	kaplan.com
American Public University	apus.edu
Pearson Education	pearsoned.com

LA Tutor	latutors123.com
Proximity Learning	proxlearn.com
Revolution Prep	revolutionprep.com
Teacher Pay Teachers	teacherspayteachers.com
Tutor Hunt	tutorhunt.com
Yup	yup.com
Skill Share	skillshare.com
Take Lessons	takelessons.com
Thumb Tack	thumbtack.com
Udemy	udemy.com

Engineering

Positions in this category include different engineering and technical fields.

Company Name	Website
BASF	basf.com
Well Point	wellpoint.com
Autodesk	autodesk.com
Canonical	canonical.com
Unisys	unisys.com
Hitachi	hitachi.com

| Kimberly Clark | kimberly-clark.com |

General Administration

Positions in the administration category include data entry, appointment setting, clerical, virtual assistance and more.

Company Name	Website
Aegis People Support	peoplesupport.com
Applied Card Systems	appliedcard.com
eaHelp	eahelp.com
Virtual Gal Friday	virtualgalfriday.com
Zirtual	zirtual.com
The Hartford	thehartford.com
Quest Diagnostics	questdiagnostics.com
Key For Cash	keyforcash.com
Lifebushido	lifebushido.com
Pacific Market research	pacificmarketresearch.com
American Public University System	apus.edu
Lunex	lunextelecom.com

Michigan First Credit Union	michiganfirstcareers.com
Quicken Loans	quickenloanscareers.com
Dion Data Solution	diondatasolutions.net
Troy Research	troyresearch.com
Express World Brand	express.com
24/7 Virtual Assistant	247virtualassistants.com
Tpo Brain Trust	tpo-inc.com
Blue Zebra Appointment Setters	bluezebraappointmentsetting.com
Dei Studios	devistudios.com
Mountain West Communications	mountainwest.com
Mulberry Studio Inc.	mulberrystudio.com
Humanatic	humanatic.com
The Pincushion	pincushion.needle.com
Short Task	shorttask.com
The Chat Shop	thechatshop.com
Axion Data Service	axiondata.com
ADP	jobs.adp.com
Overland solutions	olsi.net
Pay Junction	payjunction.com
IBM	ibm.com

SalesForce	salesforce.com
About.com	About.com
Aon	aon.com
Adobe Systems	adobe.com
Clarity Consultants	clarityconsultants.com
PAREXEL	parexel.com
BroadSpire	broadspire.com
Infor	infor.com
Thomson Reuters	thomsonreuters.com
AmerisourceBergen	amerisourcebergen.com
Contemporary Virtual Assistant	cva.bamboohr.com/jobs/
Fiserv	fiserv.com
BCD Travel	bcdtravel.com
CareFusion	carefusion.com
AIG	aig.com
Express Scripts	express-scripts.com
Nielsen	nielsen.com
Quintiles	quintiles.com
ICF International Inc.	icfi.com
Kronos Incorporated	kronos.com

Assistant Match	assistantmatch.com
Red Butler	redbutler.com
Active Network	activenetwork.com
SigTrack	sigtrack.net
Time Etc	timeetc.com
Vasumo	vasumo.com
Case Information System	cassinfo.com

Marketing

Positions in this category include advertising and marketing.

Company Name	Website
CyberCoder	cybercoders.com
SAP	sap.com
Red Hat	redhat.com
Cargill	cargill.com

Medical

The positions in this category include nurses, researchers and clinical trial studies.

Company Name	Website
Fonemed	fonemed.com
United Healthcare	unitedhealthgroup.com
SHS Inc	shsinc.com
Insurance Recruiting & Executive Search	iresinc.com
Humana	humana.com
Clinical Connection	clinicalconnection.com
Axion	axionllc.com
Healthcare Recruiters Int'l	hcrintl.com
eAssist Dental Billing	dentalbilling.com
Aetna	aetna.com
Westat	westat.com
McKesson Corporation	mckesson.com
Pharmaceutical Development	ppdi.com
Optum	optum.com
Zimmer	zimmer.com
Dignity Health	dignityhealth.org
Health Net	healthnet.com
Novartis	novartis.com
Alere	alere.com

National Cancer Institute	cancer.gov
National Institute of Mental Health	nimh.nih.gov
CISCRP	ciscrp.org
National Institute of Health	clinicalstudies.info.nih.gov
Care.com	care.com
Honor	joinhonor.com
Carenet	carenethealthcare.com

Modeling Agencies

Modeling agencies for both children and adults.

Company Name	Website
Green Agency	greenagency.com
Irene Marie	irenemarie.com
Michele Pommier	michelepommier.com
Wilhelmina Models	wilhelmina.com
World of Kids Inc	worldofkidsagency.com
CESD Talent Agency	cesdtalent.com
Ford Models	fordmodels.com
Funny Face Talent Inc.	fftmodels.com
Generation	generationmm.com
Gilla Roos	gillaroosmiami.com

Notary Public

A notary public takes an oath with their state's office. They get paid for their signature and notarizing different documents. The companies below contract notaries.

Company Name	Website
American Signing Connection	americansigningconnection.com
First American Mortgage	famortgageservices.com
State Wide Document Service	statewidedocuments.com
America's Best Closers	americasbestclosers.com
The Mobile Notary	themobilenotary.com
Go Mobile Notary	gomobilenotary.com
123 Notary	123notary.com
Notary Rotary	notaryrotary.com

Paid Survey

Some surveys, NOT ALL, may require you to use a credit card and go through a trial period and then cancel. Your credit card won't get charged, if you cancel within the trial period and you will be paid upon completion of that period. You must follow the guidelines in order to receive credit for the assignment.

Company Name	Website
The African American Voice	theafricanamericanvoice.com
American Consumer Opinion	acop.com
I-say	i-say.com
Opinion Out Post	opinionoutpost.com
Survey Saanvi	survey.saanvi.org
Survey Savvy	surveysavvy.com
Focus Group	focusgroup.com
Vindale Research	vindale.com
Epoll	epollsurveys.com
Permission Research	permissionresearch.com
Slice The Pie	slicethepie.com

Photography/Paparazzi

Listed below are websites where you can sale your pictures and photography.

Company Name	Website
X17	X17online.com
Splash News and Picture agency	splashnews.com
The Snitcher Desk	thesnitcherdesk.com
Obeo	obeo.com
The Sun Magazine	rsmadness.com
Tour This Place	tourthisplace.com
Victory Productions	victoryprd.com

Secret Shopper

Secret shopping, mystery shopping and/or quality assurance agents perform many different duties. Some duties include: checking the quality of customer service, food, and observing fair consumer practices.

Company Name	Website
Ellis Property Management	epmsonline.com
Amusement Advantage	amusementadvantage.com
A Closer Look	a-closer-look.com
Anonymous Insights	a-insights.com
Bare International	bareinternational.com
Ardent Services	ardentservices.com

At Your Service Marketing	aysm.com
Informa Research	informars.com
Best Mark	bestmark.com
Market Force	marketforce.com
Consumer Impressions Inc	consumerimpressions.com
Customer First	customer-1st.com
CSE	customerserviceexperts.com
Sparks Research	sparksresearch.com
DSG Associates	dsgai.com
Northwest Loss Prevention	nwlpc.com
Imyst Mystery Shopping	imyst.com
Jancyn	jancyn.com
KSS International	kernscheduling.com
LeBlanc & Associates	mleblanc.com
Melinda Brody & Company	melindabrody.com
Mystery Shoppers Inc	mystery-shoppers.com
Pacific Research Group	pacificresearchgroup.com
Promotion Network	promotionnetworkinc.com
Quality Assessment	qams.com
Quality Assurance	qacinc.com

Coyle Hospitality	coylehospitality.com
Quest for the Best	questforbest.com
Ritter Associates	ritterassociates.com
Rocky Mountain Merchandising	rockymm.com
RQA Inc	rqa-inc.com
Second To None	second-to-none.com
Service Check	servicecheck.com
Service Evaluation Concepts	serviceevaluation.com
Service Impressions	serviceimpressions.com
Experience Exchange	serviceintelligence.com
Service Performance Group	spgweb.com
Pehrson WEb	pwgroup.com
Field Agent app	fieldagent.net
The Solomon Group	thesolomongroup.com
Spies In Disguise	spiesindisguise.com
Onsource	onsourceonline.com
Call Center QA	callcenterqa.org
isecretshop	isecretshop.com
DBS Marketing	bdsmktg.com

Roadside Assistance

Roadside agent's assist customers with towing, flat tires, fuel, jump starts, lock outs, and minor auto repairs. Roadside agents can do these services independently and/or be contracted through companies like AT&T, Allstate, AARP, AAA and many others. The following websites contract roadside agents to assist major companies with their clients

Company Name	Website
Best Roadside Service	bestroadsideservice.com
Asurion	asurion.com
Signature Motor Club	sigmotorclub.com
Agero	agero.com
Popalock Locksmith	popalock.com

Telephone Actor

This category includes telephone actors who verbally act out a caller's fantasies. Individuals paid to sit in a studio audience are also included in this category.

Company Name	Website
Phone Actress	phone-actress.com
On Site Productions	onsetproductions.com
SoneFex Inc	sonefex.com
Symmetry Concepts	symmetrygirls.com
Pay Per Call	paypercall.com
1800 Delilah	1800delilah.com
Lip Service	lipservice.net
Text121	text121chat.com
Nite Flirt	niteflirt.com
Standing Room Only	standingroomonly.tv
New York Show Tickets	nytix.com
The Snuggle Buddies	snugglebuddies.com

Transcriptionist and Coder

They turn audio into text and generate billing-ready documents for hospitals and clinics.

Company Name	Website
Expedict	expedict.com
Mulberry Studio Inc	mulberrystudio.com
Net Transcripts	nettranscripts.com

Quick Tate	typists.quicktate.com
Speak Write	speakwrite.com
Team Double-Click	teamdoubleclick.com
Tigerfish	tigerfish.com
Accentance	accentance.com
Accu Tran Global	accutranglobal.com
A.D. Secretarial Service Inc	alicedarling.com
American High-Tech	htsteno.com
Cambridge Transcriptionists	ctran.com
Cyber Dictate	cyberdictate.com
Modern Day Scribe LLC	moderndayscribe.com
Verbal Ink	verbalink.com
Neal R. Gross & Co., Inc	nealrgross.com
Net Transcripts	nettranscripts.com
Perfect Transcription	perfecttranscription.com
Task	usetask.com
Transcription 2000	transcription-services.org
Transcription Services Inc	tsitranscripts.com
Type Write Word Processing Service	typewp.com
Ubiqus	ubiqus.com

Viable Technologies	viabletek.com
Alice Darling Secretarial service	alicedarling.com
Production Transcripts	productiontranscripts.com

The Coding Network LLC	codingnetwork.com
Acceptance	accentance.com
M Modal	mmodal.com
Fantastic Transcripts	fantastictranscripts.com
Modern Day Scribe	moderndayscribe.com
Nuance Transcription Services	nuance-nts.com
Mag Mutal	magmutual.com
M Modal	medquist.com
Pioneer Transcription Service	pioneer-transcription-services.com
NJPR Hospital Support Service	njpr.com
Oracle Transcription Inc.,	oracletranscription.com
Mass Transcription	masstranscription.com
Phoenix MedCom	phoenixmedcom.com
Precyse	precyse.com
ASC Services	emediamillworks.com
Specta Medi	spectramedi.com

Steno Med Inc.,	stenomed.com
Thomas Transcription Services Inc.	thomastx.com
Torres Lich & Associates Inc	torres-lich.com
Health Clinical Documentation Sol.	inhealthcds.com
Amphion Medical Solutions	amphionmedical.com
Applied Medical Services	appliedmedicalservices.com
eTranscription Solutions	etranscriptionsolutions.org
Express Document Services	expressdocumentservice.com
Fantastic Transcripts	fantastictranscripts.com
eAssist Dental Billing	dentalbilling.com

Translators

They translate one language into another in different environments such as hospitals, court rooms, airports, and other locations.

Company Name	Website
Accurapid Language Service	accurapid.com
African Translation	africantranslation.com
Bilingual America	bilingualamerica.com
Bridge	bridge.edu

Cultural link	theculturalink.com
Global Like Translations	globalinktranslations.com
Language Translation Inc.,	languagetranslation.com
Language Line Service	languageline.com
Languages Unlimited	languagesunlimited.com
Linguistic Systems Inc.,	linguist.com
Federal Bureau of Investigation	fbijobs.gov
New World Language Services Inc.,	newworldlanguages.com
Open World Multi-Lingual Services	openworldtranslations.com
ABC Translation Service	translationsabc.com
SDL	sdl.com
U C Translators	uctranslations.com
We Translate	we-translate.com
Linguist List	Linguistlist.org
Academic Word	academicword.com
Berlitz	berlitz.com
Creative English Solution	englishsolutions.ca
Lionbridge	lionbridge.com
Network Omni	networkomni.com
Patent Translators	patenttranslations.com

Telelanguage	telelanguage.com
Win Translation	wintranslation.com
Appen ButlerHill	appen.com
Pacific Interpreters	pacificinterpreters.com

Web Designers/Web Tester

The below list consists of companies that hire website designers and website testers. They pay individuals to try their websites to ensure functionality.

Company Name	Website
Ambrosia Software Inc	ambrosiasw.com
Fuze	ifuze.com
Leap Force	leapforceathome.com
BioWare	bioware.com
Appen	appen.com
User Testing	usertesting.com
Computer Sciences Corporation	csc.com
Art & Logic app Development	artlogic.com

Ask Dr. Tech	askdrtech.com
Corp Images	corpimages.net
Lion Bridge	lionbridge.com
Driver Guide	members.driverguide.com
First Beat Media	firstbeatmedia.com
Laboratory Expertise Center	labexpertise.com
My SQL	mysql.com
Plum Choice	plumchoice.com
User Centered Web Solutions	u-cwebs.com
Virtue Group	virtuogroup.com
V Worker	vworker.com
Support.com Personal Tech Experts	support.com
Lovell Technologies	lovelltechnology.com
iSoft Stone	issworld.isoftstone.com
What Users Do	whatusersdo.com

Company Name	Website
Enrolled	enrollapp.com
Try Mu UI	trymyui.com
Userlytics	userlytics.com
Alchemic Dream	alchemicdream.com
Art and Logic	artandlogic.com
Zero Chaos	zerochaos.com

Other/ Miscellaneous

Industries that did not fall into the above categories, such as skincare, admissions representative, athletic recruiter and job search websites that display work-from-home opportunities are listed below.

Company Name	Website
Admission Consultants	admissionsconsultants.com
Erie Insurance	erieinsurance.com
Face the World Foundation	facetheworld.org
Recruit	recruitzone.com
Rodan & Field Dermatologist	rodanandfields.com
Dogvacay	rover.com

Kirkus	kirkusreviews
Live World	liveworld.com
Highmark	Highmark.com
Convergence Marketing	convergencemktg.com
Hallmart cards	www.hallmark.com/online/careers
Baremetrics	baremetrics.io
Stewart Title Guaranty Company	stewart.com
Click and Work	clicknwork.com
US Department of Transpiration	dot.gov
Filmless	filmless.com
Doggy BnB	doggybnb.com
Rover	rover.com
Swifto	swifto.com
Luxe	luxe.com
Flip Key	rentals.tripadvisor.com
Home Away	homeaway.com
One Fine Stay	onefinestay.com
Coachup	coachup.com

Please note, I am not guaranteeing that the companies listed are currently hiring. Nor am I guaranteeing anyone employment.

REMEMBER, always protect yourself from scams. You should not have to pay anyone for employment or to hire you. You may be asked to cover the cost of a background check or drug screening. Use your best judgment. Although I screened these websites, please do not assume that just because a company appears in this list that they have current openings for home-based workers. PLEASE NOTE: I cannot guarantee the legitimacy of any link, company, hirer, etc. Jobseekers are strongly advised to perform their own due diligence on any company they may consider for employment.

Entrepreneurship

"The critical ingredient is getting off your butt and doing something. It's as simple as that. A lot of people have ideas, but there are few who decide to do something about them now. Not tomorrow. Not next week. But today. The true entrepreneur is a doer, not a dreamer."
-Nolan Bushnell, entrepreneur.

An entrepreneur is a person who organizes and manages a business and assumes the risk for it. Selling your own products and services can help you reach your financial goals. Starting your own business can be an exhilarating and rewarding experience. Being an entrepreneur means you are your own boss, you set your own schedule and you can make a living doing something you love.

"Entrepreneurship is neither a science nor an art. It is a practice."
- Peter Drucker, educator, and author.

What do you love doing? What are your talents and abilities? Have you discovered what you are good at? If not, do not worry! Take your time, think about it. Finding what you are good at may require a lot of thought. Think about what you enjoy doing the most. Think about what you occasionally do for free because you enjoy doing it.

* Fixing cars,
* Home repair,
* Doing hair,
* Applying makeup,
* Writing,
* Cooking,
* Party planning,
* Gardening
* Picking out clothes and/or jewelry,
* Cleaning up,
* Giving advice,

* Watching kids,

* Preaching,

* Teaching,

* Medicine, natural or otherwise.

* Exercise

   Etc……………………………….

Your gift will make room for you and it will lead you to the right people. Take your time and mediate on finding your gift. We are all born with gifts. It is up to us to discover them and use them.

Becoming a successful entrepreneur requires planning, creativity and work. Answer the following questions to gauge where you are in starting a business.

1. Do you have the perseverance to make your business a success?
2. What kind of business do you want?

3. What products and services will your business provide?

4. How much will it cost you to get started?

5. What are your prices?

6. How are your products and/or services different from your competitor's?

7. How will you advertise/promote your business?

> *"I've missed more than 9,000 shots in my career. I've lost almost 300 games. 26 times I've been trusted to take the game's winning shot and missed. I've failed over and over and over again in my life and that's why I succeed."*
> - <u>Michael Jordan</u>, NBA Hall of Famer.

To have a successful business you must plan and prepare. Research your industry, plan again, and execute. Let us go through the steps together.

<u>1) Plan your business:</u>

This should include the answers to the above questions. Your plan should contain all your business details such as your products, services, locations and target markets. It will contain your strategies and goals. If you don't have a plan written down, start now.

2) Research your business:

After you have drafted your business plan, thoroughly research your business. What caused businesses like yours to fail or succeed in the past? How can you start from the very basics? How to build clientele in your industry? What equipment is needed? How much money is needed to achieve your short-term goals and long-term goals?

3) Revise your business plan:

Adjust your original business plan to include any new developments from your research.

4) Execute your business:

This is the time to execute your plan. Start contacting the necessary people and start selling your goods and services.

> *"There's nothing wrong with staying small. You can do big things with a small team."*
> - <u>Jason Fried</u>, founder of 37signal.

      With proper planning and execution, you can start your business with little initial investment. Starting your business from the ground up is the only way you can start a business with little startup cash. Starting from the basics means building clientele and a trustworthy reputation first. Continue to obtain and maintain a dedicated customer base. Start building your business upward slowly and affordably. Build your business one goal at a time. It would not be the best decision to take out a loan for a building before you have customers. Build and maintain your clientele and a good business reputation. Think clientele, clientele. Excellent customer service is imperative. Success depends on many things, but most importantly, it depends on the support of people. And people love great customer service.

      Once your business plan is in order, it is time to come up with a name for your business. I am sure you already have a few in mind. Go to your state's official government website (statename.gov) to check if your business name is available. It is a free service and its typically called a business entity search. Once you find an available business name, you can begin legalizing your business. Fill out the proper state forms. If you need help visit www.georgepublishing.com. After your business is registered with your state, you can get an Employer Identification Number (EIN) from the IRS. With an EIN number, you can file business taxes, open a business bank account and apply for loans and credit. An EIN number is your business's social security number.

This is a great start, if you need help legalizing your business visit www.georgepublishing.com. Good luck on your journey to success.

"The best time to plant a tree was 20 years ago. The second best time is now."
- <u>Chinese proverb</u>.

Job Searching Techniques

Searching and applying for a new job is a job within itself. You must dedicate at least two hours per day to job searching. Today, the application process is online. The online application process can be very tedious and time-consuming. It takes about 30-45 minutes to fill out an online application. It takes this long because you must complete the registration process, set your personal profile, upload your resume and fill in your data. Be patient. I recommend that you take a break before you fill out each application to refresh your mind. Collect your thoughts to help you clearly communicate your skills to the employer. Try to fill out two applications per day. Spending two to three hours a day seeking employment will increase your odds of finding a job that you like.

Only fill out applications for positions that you are qualified for. You do not want to waste your time filling out applications for positions you don't have the education and/or experience for. You don't want to take time away from positions that you qualify for.

When searching online for jobs, try to stay away from commonly-known job search databases like monster.com, careerbuilder.com indeed.com and wanted.com. These sites are flooded with people applying for the same positions. Who knows how often these websites update their database. It is a total waste of time applying for a position that is already filled. This is likely to happen on a talent bank. I am not discrediting these websites. They are helpful resources and can help you to find job leads. People and companies use these websites all the time. Try using different techniques and you will get different results.

When looking for a new employer, you should think outside of the box. Be aware of your surroundings. Pay attention to the things you purchase, eat, and pass by. Research the name of the company you see on labels and check if they are hiring. Look around at skyscrapers and see if you might notice a company's name, look them up and check their career page. Keep a note pad in your car or with you, so when you find a company you never heard of write it down and Google it later. You will find that there are thousands of careers you can choose from. Search all companies you are unfamiliar with, no matter how big or small. There is a potential for employment with any company.

When searching a company online, browse their career page to see if they are hiring. Also, it doesn't hurt to do things the old-fashioned way and call the company or walk-in to find out if they are hiring.

If you have a degree, trade, or you just want to start a new career, remember there is nothing wrong with starting from the bottom and working your way up in a company to gain experience. Work experience is just as valuable as an education. If you are serious about pursuing a new career, you can't be afraid to learn new things.

knowledge

Résumé Writing Tips

Contrary to what some may think, résumés are still very valuable. Although your online profiles, networks and uploads are important, your résumé is the key factor. Your resume is a synopsis of what you have accomplished. Do not simply rely on online publishing platforms as a way for companies to find you. Recruiters are looking at hundreds of applications, so your résumé is the key factor that separates you from the rest of the applicants.

Your résumé should be unique for each position you apply for. Do not use a generic résumé. Structure your résumé to highlight your strengths. If your experience looks better than your education, list it first. There is no written rule for résumé structure, as long as your contact information is on top and your objective is clear. Try this format for your résumé:

1st- Your contact information. Your name, email address, and telephone number.

2nd- Your objective, this should be tailored to each position you are applying for. Include the company's name and position you are seeking.

3rd- Highlight what the employer is looking for. This would be your work history or education.

4th- Anything else you would like to add, such as additional skills, certificates, and other accomplishments.

The verbiage on your résumé is what gets you in the door for your interview. No misspelled words, no slang. Simple changes like replacing your job title from cashier to sales associate or from stocker to inventory control specialist make your résumé more appealing. I suggest looking up your past job titles to see how other companies describe it. That way you will have a refreshed description for your previous job functions.

Your résumé should not exceed one page, nor should it be any less. Employers review a lot of résumés. Many employers don't read past the first five lines of a résumé. Avoid having a lot of blank spaces on your résumé. You can always add to your résumé in hopes to sell yourself to your future employer. If you don't have much experience or education, the extra blank space is your opportunity to be creative. You can add volunteer work, additional skills and abilities you feel are important. Blank spaces make you seem inexperienced and unenthusiastic. Look at the résumé examples on the following pages. Both are for the same position and with the same experience. Compare the résumés. Neither are right or wrong, because there isn't a specific format for résumé writing. Which do you prefer? The first one is generic and the second one has more details.

STARTING NOW!

John Doe
123 Happy St.
Anytown, Mi. 99995
313-555-1212

Education:

12/2017 – Present   University of Education
Business.

8/95-6/99   Academy high school
Received Diploma

Experience:

2/2008- 4/2018   The Convenience Store
Cashier
Responsibilities: Cash handling and sales.

10/2007- 2/2008   Call Center Inc.
Customer Service Representative.
Responsibilities: Inbound and outbound call taking. Customer service and sales.

12/2002-8/2004   Retail Store
Greeter
Responsibilities: Welcomed customers into the store and answered customer questions.

John Doe
123 Happy St.
Anytown, Mi. 99995
313-555-1212

Objective: To obtain a fulltime position as cashier at The Specialty Store.

Summary of Qualifications

- Excellent sales and customer service skills.
- Experience processing payments.
- Enthusiastic contributor and supporter of team goals.

Employment History

2/2008-4/2018   The Convenience Store
Title: **Customer Service and Sales Representative**
Responsibilities: Processed payments and handled cash in accordance with the companies accounting procedures and policies. Completed cashier reports, resolved any discrepancies.

10/2007-8/2008   Call Center Inc.
Title: **Customer Service Representative**
Responsibilities: Inbound and outbound customer service and sales calls. Ensured all calls were handled according to policies, procedures, and quality standards. Maintained monthly sales goals.

12/2004-8/2004   Retail Store
Title: **Customer Service Representative**
Responsibilities: Greeted customers to find out their needs. Recommended, selected and helped customers locate the right merchandise. Described product features and benefits. Answered customer questions.

Education

12/2017- Current   **University of Education**
Bachelor of Business Administration, Degree anticipated May 2020.

8/95-6/99   **Academy high school**
Received Diploma

Additional Abilities and Skills

Microsoft Word, PowerPoint, Excel, and Publisher. WPM 45.
Internet proficient. Prioritize workload, and problem-solving skills.

Traditional Careers In-Demand

This section of the book discusses careers that are currently in demand. The manual lists specific careers, gives a brief description of the job function, education needed, approximate salary, and helpful website links for additional research.

If you are a senior in high school, you can browse this section to help guide you in making decisions for your future goals. If you are a current college student or an adult professional looking for a career change, this section can give you direction. Below, in alphabetical order, is a list of careers that are in demand and growing over the next few years. This information is based on the data collected by the United States Bureau of Labor and Statistics.

Able Seaman/ Merchant Mariner

Description: Being an Able Seaman is similar to being a truck driver. Instead of transporting objects on the road, you are transporting them through the water. Some Seaman spend extended periods of time at sea and some go home every night. It all depends on the assignment. Seaman move large amounts of cargo, as well as passengers across waterways. Positions as a seaman vary depending on experience and training. They include, but are not limited to, Captain, Deck officer, Deck hand, Pilot, Ship engineer, Marine oiler, and Motor boat Operator.

Education: Education and training for seaman is regulated by the United States Coast Guard. Entry level positions require first aid and firefighting education. Some positions require certain credentials such as, Transportation Workers Identification (TWIC) and Merchant Mariners (MMC).

Pay: $30,000 to $103,000 + annually depending on position and training.

For more information:
www.marad.dot.gov
www.uscg.mil/nmc
www.americanwaterways.com

Actuary

Description: Actuaries assess the risk for different products and services for insurance companies. They determine how much people pay for insurance premiums. They usually work with numbers and are good in mathematics, probability and general statistics.

Education: A Bachelor's Degree in any background is required. A mathematics background is preferred but not required. Actuaries must pass a series of four exams. Income is evaluated based on the number of exams passed. Exams can be self-studied.

Pay: $50,000 to over $500,000+ annually depending on the number of tests passed.

For more information visit:
www.beanactuary.org
www.dwsimpson.com

Agricultural and Food Scientist

Description: Food scientists study farm crops and animals to develop ways of improving their quality and quantity. They play an important role in maintaining the nation's food supply.

Education: Bachelor's degree in Agricultural Science.

Pay: $50,000 to $105,000 annually.

For more information:
www.ift.org
www.agronomy.org
www.crops.org
www.soils.org

Aircraft and Avionic Equipment Mechanics and Service Technicians

Description: Individuals in this field are responsible for airplane maintenance. They inspect aircraft engines, landing gears, brakes and other parts of an aircraft.

Education: High school diploma and must be a certified mechanic by the Federal Aviation Administration (FAA).

Pay: $20.00 to $31.00 hourly.

For more information:
www.pama.org
www.faa.gov

Aircraft Pilots and Flight Engineers

Description: Pilots are highly trained professionals who fly airplanes or helicopters to carry out a wide variety of tasks. Most are airline pilots, co-pilots, and flight engineers who transport passengers and cargo.

Education: Pilots must have a commercial pilot's license.

Pay: $45,680 to $150,480 annually.

For more information:
www.faa.gov
www.rotor.com
www.clearedtodream.org

Air Traffic Controller:

Description: Air Traffic Controllers ensure the safe operations of all aircrafts. They work with the national airspace system to coordinate the movement of air traffic. They are the policemen in the sky.
Education: GED or High school diploma required. Passing of the FAA authorized pre-employment test.

Pay: $45,000 to $111,870 annually.

For more information:
www.faa.gov
www.natca.org

Archivists, Curators, and Museum Technicians

Description: Archivists, curators, and museum technicians work for museums, governments, zoos, colleges, universities, corporations, and other institutions that require experts to preserve important records and artifacts. These workers preserve important objects and documents, including works of art, transcripts of meetings, photographs, coins, stamps, and historic objects.

Education: Bachelors or a graduate degree in history or library science.

Pay: $26,600 to $90,205 annually.

For more information:
www.conservation-us.org
www.aam-us.org
www.archivists.org
www.certifiedarchivists.org
www.nagara.org

Armed Forces

Description: The military provides training and work experience in fields for more than 2.4 million people. Individuals serve in the Army, Navy, Marine Corps, Air Force, Reserves and Army National Guard.

Education: To join the military, applicants must meet age, educational, aptitude, physical, and character requirements.

Pay: First year varies depending on specialty and department; varies from $28,377 to $50,000 annually.

For more information:

www.todaysmilitary.com

Audiologists

Description: Audiologists work with people who have hearing, balance, and other ear-related difficulties. They examine individuals of all ages and identify symptoms of hearing loss and other neural issues.

Education: Master's degree in audiology

Pay: $40,360 to $98,880 annually.

For more information visit:
www.asha.org
www.audfound.org

Automotive Service Technicians and Mechanics

Description: Mechanics inspect, maintain, and repair automobiles and light trucks. They perform basic car maintenance, such as oil changes and tire rotations. They diagnose more complex problems, plan, and execute vehicle repairs.

Education: Automotive Service Excellence (ASE) certification.

Pay: $12.44 to $22.64 hourly.

For more information visit:
www.autocareerstoday.org
www.natef.org
www.ayes.org

Billboard Posterers/ Painter and paper hangers

Description: They remove old materials and prepare surfaces to be papered; they attach advertising posters on surfaces such as walls and billboards.

Education: High School diploma, and/or on-the-job training.

Pay: $13.00 to 28.00 hourly.

For more information visit:
www.lamar.com
www.outfrontmedia.com
www.nccer.org

Brick Masons, Block Masons, and Stonemasons

Description: For thousands of years, these workers have built buildings, roads, walkways, and walls using bricks, concrete blocks, and natural stone. This position will continue to be in demand for years to come.

Education: On-the-job training, some technical and vocational schools offer classes.

Pay: $11.63 to $31.87 hourly.

For more information visit:
www.masoncontractors.org
www.imiweb.org
www.ncma.org

Broadcast and Sound Engineering Technicians and Radio Operators

Description: The duties of an engineer and operator in this field include setting up and maintaining the electrical equipment used in radio and television broadcasts, concerts, plays, sound recordings, and movies.

Education: An Associates degree in broadcast technology, electronics, computer networking, or a related field is generally recommended.

Pay: $30,000 to $90,000 annually.

For more information:
www.nab.org
www.sbe.org
www.infocomm.org

Bus Drivers

Description: Bus drivers provide transportation for millions of people, from commuters, school children and vacationers. They transport people city to city, state to states and cross country.

Education: High school diploma and commercial driver's licenses (CDL) with the proper endorsements.

Pay: $12.79 to $26.74 hourly.

For more information visit:
www.fmcsa.dot.gov
www.nasdpts.org
www.yellowbuses.org
www.uma.org

Cardiovascular Technologists and Technicians

Description: Cardiovascular technologists and technicians schedule appointments, review physicians' interpretations and patient files. Technicians specialize in electrocardiograms and stress testing.

Education: Associates degree.

Pay: $32,800 to $74,760+ annually

For more information:
www.caahep.org
www.svunet.org
www.cci-online.org
www.ardms.org

Cargo and Freight Agents

Description: Cargo and Freight agents help transportation companies manage incoming and outgoing shipments in airlines, trains, trucking terminals and shipping docks. Agents expedite shipments by determining a route and preparing necessary documents.

Education: High school diploma and on the job training.

Pay: $13.67 to $27.70 hourly

For more information visit:
www.tianet.org

Chefs

Description: Chefs oversee the daily food service operation of a restaurant or other food service establishments.

Education: Associates or bachelor's degree in hospitality or culinary arts.

Pay: $29,050 to $66,680+ annually.

><u>For more information:</u>
>www.restaurant.org
>www.acfchefs.org
>www.personalchef.com

Chemists and Materials Scientists

Description: Chemists and Materials Scientists search for new knowledge about chemicals and use it to improve life. Chemical research has led to the discovery and development of new and improved synthetic fibers, paints, adhesives, drugs, cosmetics, electronic components, lubricants, and thousands of other products.

Education: A bachelor's degree in chemistry or a related discipline.

Pay: $48,630 to $124,010 annually

><u>For more information:</u>
>www.acs.org

Chiropractors

Description: Chiropractors diagnose and treat patients with health problems in the musculoskeletal system. Many chiropractors treat and deal specifically with the spine and the manipulation of the spine.

Education: Chiropractors must be licensed, with an Associates or Bachelors degree.

Pay: $45,540 to $96,700 annually

For more information:
www.acatoday.org
www.chiropractic.org
www.cce-usa.org
www.fclb.org
www.nbce.org

Clinical Laboratory Technologists and Technicians

Description: Clinical laboratory personnel examine and analyze body fluids, and cells. They analyze the chemical content of fluids; match blood for transfusions; and test for drug levels in the blood.

Education: A bachelor's degree in medical technology or in one of the life sciences. Clinical laboratory technicians need an associate degree or a certificate.

Pay: $36,180 to $74,680 annually

For more information visit:
www.naacls.org
www.aabb.org
www.cytopathology.org

Computer Network, Systems, and Database Administrators

Description: They set up, test, and evaluate systems such as local area network, wide area networks, the Internet, intranets, and other data communication systems.

Education: Associates degree or professional certification.

Pay: $41,000 to $104,070 annually

For more information:
www.lopsa.org
www.dama.org

www.computer.org

Computer Software Engineers and Computer Programmers

Description: They apply the theories and principles of computer science and mathematical analysis to create, test, and evaluate the software applications and systems that make computers work.

Education: Bachelor's degree in software engineering, computer science or a related field

Pay: $67,790 to $135,780+ annually

For more information:
www.computingcareers.acm.org
www.computer.org

Computer Support Specialists

Description: Provides technical assistance, support, and advice to individuals and organizations that depend on information technology.

Education: Associate degree or certification.

Pay: $33,680 to $70,750 annually.

For more information:
www.asponline.com

Computer Systems Analyst

Description: They design and develop new computer systems.

Education: Bachelor's degree in management information systems.

Pay: $58,460 to $118,440 annually

For more information:

www.computingcareers.acm.org
www.computer.org

Conservation Scientist and Forester

Description: Conservation scientists and foresters manage the use and development of forests, rangelands, and other natural resources.

Education: A bachelor's degree in forestry, biology, natural resource management, or environmental sciences.

Pay: $42,980 to $86,910+ annually.

For more information:
www.safnet.org
www.forestguild.org
www.rangelands.org

Construction and Building Inspectors

Description: Examine buildings, highways, streets, sewers, water systems, dams, bridges, and other structures. They comply with building codes and ordinances.

Education: High school diploma and passing a state approved examination.

Pay: $31,270 to 80,000 annually.

For more information visit:
www.ashi.org
www.iccsafe.org
www.nahi.org

Construction Equipment Operator

Description: Construction equipment operators use machinery to move construction materials at construction sites.

Education: Commercial driver's license, high school diploma, on the job training.

Pay: $12.47 to $60.00 hourly.

For more information visit:
www.piledrivers.org
www.iuoe.org
www.nccco.org

Construction Laborer

Description: Assist all construction tradesmen and does general labor.

Education: High School diploma or G.E.D.

Pay: $12.00 to $20.00 hourly.

For more information visit:
www.liunatraining.org
www.nccer.org

Correctional Officers

Description: Responsible for overseeing individuals in a correctional institution.

Education: A high school diploma, and correctional officers training academy.

Pay: $28,790 to $73,630+ annually

For more information:
www.aca.org
www.aja.org
www.bop.gov

Correctional Treatment Specialists

Description: Gives counsel to offenders and create rehabilitation plans for them to follow while on parole.

Education: Bachelor's degree in social work, criminal justice, or psychology.

Pay: $45,910 to $78,210+ annually.

For more information:
www.appa-net.org

Cost Estimator

Description: Cost estimators develop the cost information that business owners and managers use to make a bid on a contract or to decide on the profitability of a new proposed project or product. They also determine which investments are making a profit.

Education: Bachelor's or associates degree in physical science, mathematics, or statistics
Pay: $33,150, to $94,470 annually.

For more information:
www.aspenational.org
www.aacei.org
www.sceaonline.org

Court Reporters or Stenographer

Description: Court reporters create verbatim transcripts of speeches, conversations, legal proceedings, meetings, and other events. Stenographers also closed caption live television programs.

Education: High school diploma and Court Reporter certified.

Pay: $35,390 to $83,500 + annually

For more information visit:
www.aaert.org
www.ncraonline.org
www.nvra.org
www.uscra.org

Diagnostic Medical Sonographer

Description: Sonography is commonly associated with ultrasound imaging during pregnancy, but this technology has many other applications in the diagnosis and treatment of medical conditions throughout the body.

Education: Certificate of completion from an accredited program.

Pay: $43,600 to $83,950 annually.

For more information:
www.sdms.org
www.ardms.org
www.aium.org
www.arrt.org

Dietitian and Nutritionist

Description: Dietitian and nutritionist plan food and nutrition programs, supervise meal preparation, and oversee meal servings. They prevent and treat illnesses by promoting healthy eating habits and by recommending dietary modifications.

Education: Bachelor's degree in dietetics, foods and nutrition, food service systems management, or a related area.

Pay: $31,460 to $73,410 + annually

For more information:
www.eatright.org
www.cdrnet.org

Drafter

Description: Prepares technical drawings and plans, which are used to build things from microchips to skyscrapers. There are different types of drafters, aeronautical, architectural and civil.

Education: Bachelors and/or Associates degree with a background in mathematics, science, computer technology or computer graphics. Armed forces training will substitute for education.

Pay: $30,000 to $79,000+ annually.

For more information visit:
www.adda.org

Education Administrator

Description: They manage the day-to-day activities in schools, daycare centers, and colleges/ universities. They also direct the educational programs of businesses, correctional institutions, museums, and community service organizations.

Education: Master's degree in education.

Pay: $54,680 to $160,500+ annually.

> **For more information visit:**
> www.aacrao.org
> www.npbea.org

Electronic Installer and repairer:

Description: Also known as field technicians. They often travel to and from locations to repair equipment and perform preventative maintenance on a regular basis.

Education: Associates degree in electronics is preferred and professional certification maybe required.

Pay: $13.48 to $33.81 + hourly.

> **For more information visit:**
> www.iscet.org

Elevator Installer and Repairer

Description: Also referred to as elevator constructors or elevator mechanics. They assemble, install, and replace elevators, escalators, chairlifts, dumbwaiters, and moving walkways.

Education: Completion of an apprenticeship program administered by the local union, the International Union of Elevator Constructors. They can also complete training programs sponsored by independent contractors.

Pay: $19.38 to $46.78+ hourly

> **For more information visit:**
> www.iuec.org
> www.naec.org

www.thyssenkruppelevator.com
www.otisworldwide.com

Embalmer

Description: Embalmers prepare the dead for burial. Most embalmers work for funeral homes, hospitals, medical schools, and morgues.

Education: On-the-job training, or an associate degree in funeral service.

Pay: $43,480+ annually.

For more information:
www.funeraleducation.org

Emergency Medical Technician

Description: Usually dispatched by 911. Emergency Medical Technicians (EMT) arrive by ambulance and are first responders to a medical scene.

Education: High school diploma and emergency medical technician training.

Pay: $12.99 to $23.77+ hourly.

For more information visit:
www.naemt.org
www.nremt.org

Environmental Scientist and Specialist

Description: They use their knowledge of the natural sciences to protect the environment. By identifying issues and finding solutions to minimize hazards to the environment and the population.

Education: A bachelor's degree in an earth science, a master's degree in environmental science or a related natural science is preferred.

Pay: $45,340 to $102,610+ annually.

For more information visit:

www.agiweb.org
www.nrep.org

Farmers, Ranchers, and Agricultural Managers

Description: They produce enough food and fiber to meet the needs of the United States and for export. Farmers and ranchers are entrepreneurs, some own and operate family owned farms.

Education: On-the-job training. An associate or bachelor's degree in agriculture.

Pay: $20,000 to $100,000+ annually.

For more information:
www.asfmra.org
www.ffa.org
www.nal.usda.gov
www.attra.ncat.org

Flight Attendant

Description: Flight Attendants ensure that security and safety regulations are followed while flying. They also try to make flights comfortable and enjoyable for passengers.

Education: High school diploma and Certification by the FAA.

Pay: $35,930 to $65,350.

For more information visit:
www.afanet.org

Funeral director

Description: Also called morticians and undertakers, they arrange the details and handle the logistics of funerals. Funeral directors establish the location, dates, memorial service, and burial.

Education: Bachelors and/or associates degree in Mortuary science.

Pay: $38,980 to $92,940+ annually.

For more information:
www.nfda.org
www.abfse.org

Hazardous Materials Removal Worker

Description: They dispose of asbestos, radioactive, nuclear, arsenic, lead, mercury and any other toxic materials. They are also called abatement, remediation, or decontamination specialists.

Education: High school diploma.

Pay: $14.09 to $30.42+ hourly.

For more information:
www.phmsa.dot.gov
www.liunatraining.org

Heavy Vehicle and Mobile Equipment Service Technician

Description: They repair and maintain engines, hydraulics, transmissions, and electrical systems for heavy duty vehicles. Farm machinery, cranes, bulldozers, and railcars are all examples of heavy duty vehicles.

Education: Completion of a formal diesel or heavy equipment mechanic training program.

Pay: $16.71 to $30.57 hourly.

For more information:
www.natef.org

Insurance Underwriter

Description: Decide whether insurance is provided, and if so, under what terms. They identify and calculate the risk of loss for policyholders.

Education: On-the-job training.

Pay: $35,010 to $99,940 annually.

For more information:

www.iii.org
www.aicpcu.org

www.cpcusociety.org

Instructional Coordinator

Description: They play a large role in improving the quality of education in the classroom. They develop curricula, select textbooks and other materials, train teachers, and assess educational programs for quality and adherence to regulations and standards. They also assist in implementing new technology in the classroom.

Education: Master's degree or higher, and a state administrator license.

Pay: $42,070 to $93,250+ annually.

For more information:
Visit your state department of education website.

Interpreter and Translator

Description: Convert spoken word into Text. For the hearing impaired, they convert spoken word into sign language.

Education: No formal education is required. The National Association of the Deaf and the Registry of Interpreters for the Deaf, offer certifications for general sign interpreters.

Pay: $28,940 to $79,865+ annually.

For more information visit
www.imiaweb.org
www.najit.org
www.rid.org

Laboratory Technician

Description: They construct, fit, maintain, and repair braces, artificial limbs, joints, arch supports, and other surgical and medical appliances. They follow what the doctor's prescription.

Education: High school diploma and on-the-job training.

Pay: $25,250 to $47,210 + annually.

For more information visit:
www.opcareers.org
www.ncope.org
www.abcop.org
www.ada.org/117.aspx

Logging Worker

Description: Logging workers harvest thousands of acres of forest each year for timber as raw materials for countless consumer and industrial products.

Education: High school diploma and on-the-job training.

Pay: $14.00 t0 $16.00 + per hour.
For more information:
www.americanloggers.com
www.afandpa.org

Medical Records and Health Information Technician

Description: They gather patients' health records and organize and manage them by ensuring its quality, accuracy, accessibility, and security.

Education: Associates degree.

Pay: $30,610 to $50,060 annually.

For more information visit:
www.cahiim.org
www.ahima.org
www.aapc.com

Meteorologist

Description: Also known as atmospheric scientists, they study the Earth's atmosphere. Meteorologists study and forecast weather patterns, allowing forecasters to better predict thunderstorms, flash floods, tornadoes, and other hazardous weather patterns.

Education: A bachelor's degree in meteorology, Atmospheric science, or another related field.

Pay: $55,140 to $127,100+ annually.

For more information:
www.ametsoc.org
www.ucar.edu/student_recruiting
www.careers.noaa.gov

Occupational Health and Safety Specialist

Description: They prevent harm to workers, property, the environment, and the public.

Education: Bachelor's degree in occupational health, safety, or a related field.

Pay: $47,490 to $93,620 annually.

For more information visit:
www.aiha.org
www.abih.org
www.bcsp.org
www.hps.org
www.osha.gov

Optician Dispenser

Description: Dispensing opticians help select and fit eyeglasses and contact lenses. They abide by the prescriptions written by ophthalmologists or optometrists.

Education: Associate degree program in opticianry.

Pay: $26,170 to $50,580 annually.

For more information visit:
www.oaa.org
www.abo.org
www.abo-ncle.org

www.nfos.org

Optometrist

Description: Also known as an eye doctors, they examine peoples' eyes to diagnose vision problems. They prescribe eyeglasses or contact lenses. They may also provide other treatments, such as vision therapy or low vision rehabilitation.

Education: Doctor of Optometry degree, from an accredited school of optometry.

Pay: $70,140 to $176,944 annually.

For more information:
www.opted.org
www.aoa.org
www.coaccreditation.com

Orthotist and Prosthetist

Description: Assist patients with conditions of the limbs and spine by fitting and preparing orthopedic braces and prostheses.

Education: Bachelor's degree.

Pay: $65,060 to $104,540 annually.

For more information visit:
www.aopanet.org
www.opcareers.org
www.abcop.org

Paralegal and Legal Assistant

Description: Paralegals and Legal assistants help lawyers prepare for closings, hearings, trials, and corporate meetings. Paralegals also organize and track files.

Education: Associate degree in paralegal studies.

Pay: $36,080 to $73,450 annually.

For more information:
www.nala.org
www.paralegals.org
www.aafpe.org
www.nals.org

Paramedic

Description: Dispatched by 911, they provide emergency care and transport the patient to a medical facility. Some paramedics work as part of a helicopter flight crew to quickly transport critically ill or injured patients.

Education: Emergency medical technician training and associate degree.

Pay: $12.99 to $23.77 + hourly.

For more information:
www.naemt.org
www.nremt.org

Pest Control Workers

Description: They remove animals from households, apartment buildings, and other structures.

Education: High school diploma and on-the-job training in pesticide safety and use.

Pay: $11.68 to $21.34 hourly.

For more information visit:
www.pestworld.org

Pharmacists

Description: They distribute prescription drugs to individuals.

Education: A license is required in all states, and a Pharm.D. degree.

Pay: $77,390 to $131,440 + annually.

For more information visit:
www.aacp.org
www.ashp.org

www.nacds.org
www.amcp.org
www.pharmacist.com
www.nabp.net

Physical Therapist Assistant and Aide

Description: They help physical therapists provide treatment to improve patient mobility.

Education: Associates degree.

Pay: $28,580 to $54,900 annually.

For more information visit:
www.apta.org

Plumber, Pipe-layer, and Pipefitter

Description: They install, maintain, and repair different types of pipe systems. Jobs varies from water, drainage, gas systems, etc.

Education: On-the-job or technical school training.

Pay: $12.84 to $27.43 + hourly.

For more information:
www.ua.org
www.mcaa.org
www.phccweb.org

Podiatrists

Description: Diagnose and treat disorders, diseases, and injuries of the foot and lower leg.

Education: 4-year podiatric college program and a passing score on the national and state examinations.

Pay: $113,560 to $114,768 annually.

For more information:
www.apma.org
www.aacpm.org

Probation Officers

Description: They supervise offenders on probation or parole through personal contact with the offenders and their families.

Education: Bachelor's degree in social work, criminal justice, psychology or related field.

Pay: $45,910 to $78,210 annually.

> **For more information:**
> www.appa-net.org

Purchasing Manager, Buyer, and Purchasing Agent

Description: Buyers purchase a vast array of farm products, durable, nondurable goods, and services for companies and institutions. They attempt to purchase the highest quality goods and services at the lowest possible cost.

Education: Bachelor's degree in business.

Pay: $36,460 to 142,550 annually.

> **For more information:**
> www.nigp.org
> www.ism.ws

Radiation Therapist

Description: Radiation therapy is used to treat cancer in the human body. As part of a medical radiation oncology team, radiation therapists use machines called linear accelerators to administer radiation treatment to patients.

Education: A Bachelor's degree, associate degree, or certificate in radiation therapy.

Pay: $59,050 to $87,910 annually.

> **For more information visit:**
> www.arrt.org
> www.asrt.org

Radiologic Technologists

Description: They perform diagnostic imaging examinations like x rays, computed tomography, magnetic resonance imaging, and mammography.

Education: Associate degree.

Pay: $35,100 to $74,970 annually.

    For more information visit:
    www.asrt.org
    www.jrcert.org
    www.arrt.org

Rail Transportation

Description: Freight railroads transport goods to destinations within the United States and to ports to be shipped abroad. Passenger railroads deliver passengers to destinations throughout the country. Subway systems move passengers within metropolitan areas.

Education: High school diploma and on-the-job training.

Pay: $13.14 to $25.59 hourly.

    For more information visit:
    www.aar.org
    www.amtrak.com
    www.ble.org
    www.utu.org

Respiratory Therapists

Description: They evaluate, treat, and care for patients with breathing or other cardiopulmonary disorders. Respiratory therapist responsibilities include respiratory care, therapeutic treatments and diagnostic procedures.

Education: Associates degree in respiratory therapy.

Pay: $44,490 to $69,800 annually.

    For more information visit:
    www.aarc.org
    www.caahep.org
    www.nbrc.org

Robotics Technician and Engineer

Description: Design, create, test and troubleshoot problems with robots.

Education: Associates degree in robot technology.

Pay: $27,410 and $71,540 annually.

> **For more information visit:**
> www.robots.net
> www.robotinfo.net
> www.fanucrobotics.com

Rodmen, Iron, and Metal Workers

Description: Place and install iron and steel beams for buildings, bridges, and other structures.

Education: Certification in welding and rigging or on-the-job training.

Pay: $12.25 to $37.04 + hourly.

> **For more information visit:**
> www.ironworkers.org
> www.ironworkers25.org
> www.agc.org

Roofer

Description: Repair and install roofs on houses and/or buildings.

Education: High school diploma or on the job training.

Pay: $12.97 to $28.46 + hourly.

> **For more information visit:**
> www.nrca.net
> www.unionroofers.com

Social Worker

Description: Social workers assist people by helping them cope with and solve issues in their everyday lives such as family and personal issues.

Education: Bachelor's degree in social work.

Pay: $31,040 to $66,430 annually.

> **For more information visit:**
> www.cswe.org

www.socialworkers.org
www.aswb.org

Speech-Language Pathologist

Description: They work with individuals with speech, rhythm and fluency issues.

Education: Master's degree in speech pathology.

Pay: $41,240 to $99,220 + annually.

For more information visit:
www.asha.org

Surgical Technologists

Description: Also known as scrubs and operating room technicians. They assist in surgical operations under the supervision of surgeons, registered nurses, or other surgical personnel. Surgical technologists are members of operating room team.

Education: Certificate of completion from an accredited 12 to 24-month program.

Pay: $32,490 to $54,300 annually.

For more information visit:
www.ast.org
www.nbstsa.org

Surveyor

Description: Also known as geomatics engineer, are responsible for measuring and mapping the Earth's surface. Surveyors establish official land, airspace, and water boundaries. They write descriptions of land for deeds, leases, and other legal documents.

Education: Bachelor's degree in geomatics, photogrammetric, geodesy or related surveying field.

Pay: $31,440 to $87,620 + annually.

For more information visit:
www.aagsmo.org

Television, Video, and Motion Picture Camera Operator and Editor

Description: Camera operators use television, video, or motion picture cameras to shoot a wide range of footage. Editors edit soundtracks, film, and video.

Education: A bachelor's degree.

Pay: $36,250 to $112,410 + annually.

For more information visit:
www.nabetcwa.org
www.cameraguild.com

Travel Agent

Description: Travel agents offer advice on destinations and arrange transportation, hotels, tours, and events for their clients.

Education: On-the-job training.

Pay: $23,940 to $47,860 + annually.

For more information visit:
www.asta.org

Truck Drivers

Description: Drivers pick up and deliver freight from one destination to another.

Education: Commercial driver's license (CDL).

Pay: $11.63 to $27.07 + hourly.

For more information visit:
www.truckline.com
www.gettrucking.com
www.ptdi.org

Umpire, and Referee

Description: They observe game plays and impose penalties for infractions in various sports. Umpires, referees, and sports officials anticipate plays, assess situations, and determine any violations in sports.

Education: Associate or bachelor's degree in physical

education, or a related field.

Pay: $40,480 to $93,710 + annually.

For more information visit:
www.naso.org

Veterinarians

Description: Treat diseases and dysfunctions of animals. They care for the health of animals in zoos, racetracks and laboratories.

Education: Doctor of veterinary medicine (D.V.M. or V.M.D.).

Pay: $46,610 to $143,660 annually.

For more information visit:
www.avma.org
www.aavmc.org

Water and Liquid Waste Treatment Plant and System Operator.

Description: Converts waste water into safe drinking water. They run the equipment, monitor and remove pollutants from the water.

Education: High School diploma, and onsite training.

Pay: $25,000 to $60,000 annually.

Check with your local water and sewerage department, for more information, also visit:
awwa.org
nrwa.org
wef.org

Welding, Soldering, and Brazing Workers

Description: Welders are tradesmen that join metals permanently. They help with shipbuilding, automobile manufacturing, and repair. Welders also connect beams in the construction of buildings, bridges, and other structures. They join pipes in pipelines, power plants and refineries.

Education: Certifications in welding and/or on the job training.

Pay: $10.50 to 25.00 + hourly.

For more information visit:
www.aws.org
www.fmanet.org

# # #

I hope you found this information to be useful. Thank you for taking the time and reading the manual. We greatly value your opinion. If you have any questions, comments or concerns, fill free to contact us at www.georgepublishing.com. Good luck on your journey into a prosperous more successful future.

Jennifer Benson
  Author
  www.jobs42day.com
  248-955-3145

Made in the USA
Columbia, SC
14 September 2018